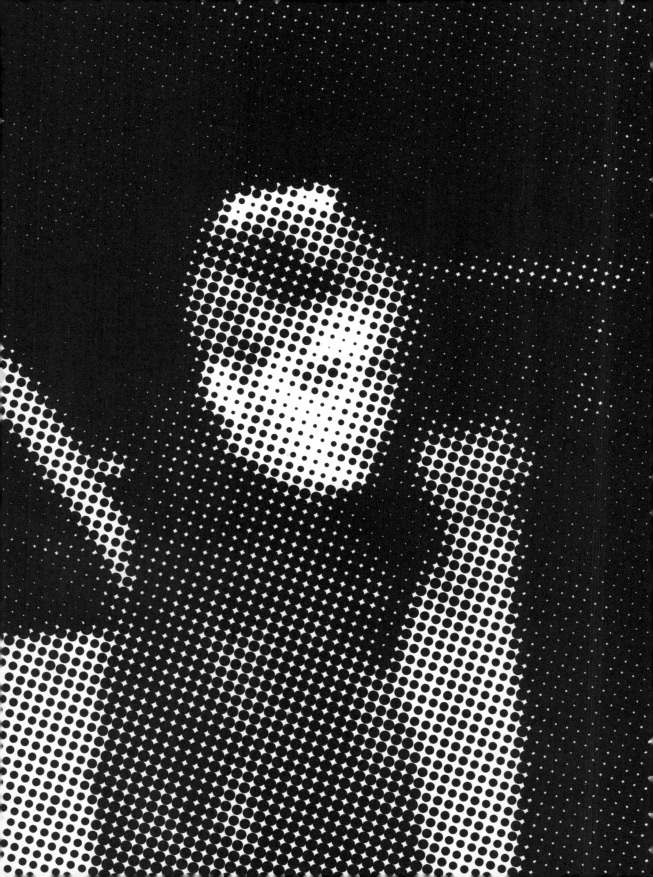

UNTYPICAL GIRLS

STYLES AND SOUNDS OF THE TRANSATLANTIC INDIE REVOLUTION

For my indie rocker yoofs,
Violet, Herbie and Marigold

Contents

Introduction:
Who Were the Untypical Girls?

Girls have been involved in bands and music from the very inception of pop music, but it was only with the advent of punk that this involvement became more than a surface presence. With a newfound sense of liberation, the untypical girls of the late '70s defiantly dictated the terms of participation, flaunting the deep-rooted chauvinism within the industry and society at large to speak out on equal terms and take control of their own musical destiny.

Untypical Girls sets out to excavate the roots of what is now universally known as indie girl style, traversing the journey from its punk genesis through the myriad '80s and early '90s indie scenes; post-punk, paisley underground, C86, shoegaze, college rock and grunge; finally culminating in riot grrrl. I've chosen a pathway that follows a transatlantic parallel between the British indie scenes and those of the USA. This captures the back and forth artistic exchange across the continents and also mirrors my personal life journey, which led me from '80s Essex and London to '90s San Francisco.

I came of age just as the British indie scenes began to crystallise in the early '80s. At countless gigs across the capital and its sprawling suburbs, I bore witness to the visual noise, noting gradual shifts in styles within the movement. Back then, the indie scene provided a true counterbalance to a mainstream, macho, dross society dominated by the aggressive, oppressive politics of Thatcher/Reagan. Obsessing over records, clothing and fanzines in a frenzy of youthful geekdom, the magnetic force of the scene was immense and life engulfing, offering a bastion of hope and poetic creativity.

At this stage, my view of the US indie scene of the mid-'80s was largely accessed via the bulging racks of obscure vinyl imports in the great West London record shop meccas of Plastic Passion, Vinyl Solution and of course, Rough Trade. Although a few of the smaller US groups toured the UK and vice versa, my indie world remained by and large a domestic cul de sac. Fanzines such as *Maximum Rock n' Roll, Forced Exposure, Flipside, Bucketful Of Brains, 99th Floor* and the hugely insightful *K Records Newsletters* helped me to gradually piece together a picture of America's vast underground landscape. Certain names of distant towns kept recurring; Washington DC, Olympia and San Francisco, in particular.

As the '80s drew to a close, the gravitational pull of the US scene was so great I decided pack up sticks and relocate. Working as a vintage clothing dealer and musician on the peripheral outer limits, I arrived in San Francisco in 1990. It was a dizzying experience; the city buzzed with DIY gigs, small indie record shops and thrift stores. Bohemia was alive and well and the indie scene was in full tilt!

The vibrant energy of the US scene of 1990 reminded me of the UK indie scenes of '85-'87. Women were at the forefront – although I was repeatedly told that it hadn't always been that way. Gradually, I realised the journeys that had been undertaken through the undefined hinterlands of post-hardcore underground college rock or by way of the fabled paisley underground. The voices I was hearing were ringing so loud and clear because they had been suppressed for so long.

I round off this story in '93 as the scene was starting to lose pace and vigour. Most of the key groups were at that stage either calling it a day or fading from relevance, sinking into a void of complacency as the 'corporate ogre' bought out the scenes wholesale, causing fractures and internal schisms that could never be fully repaired. But the 16 years spanning 1977 to 1993 will forever be the golden era of the indie scene, the golden era of the Untypical Girls.

This book is by no means an indie girl A-Z. Merely a glimpse into a journey from nascent radical stages to the full flower of revolution, the looks and attitudes of which are frighteningly relevant today. Most of the bands featured were mixed/ unisex, but to maintain the book's female focus I've featured photos of the girls only, and in some cases guys were cropped out.

Sorry chaps!

Sam Knee, 2017

UK 1977-82

Fairytale in the Supermarket

Punk exploded onto the landscape of British youth culture in 1976. Its sheer energy and rage offered a platform for disenfranchised youth of all description to kick back against the establishment. This was certainly the case for the women on the scene. In a rigged system, women in pop music had hitherto been reduced to oversexualised mouthpieces for the smug, self-satisfied men in charge. Punk offered a genuine idiom of self-expression through three-chord, two-minute wonders. A new generation of female British germ free adolescents blazed a path to liberation and self-realisation that only really reached its logical conclusion 13 years later across the Atlantic in the heady days of riot grrrl.

The first wave of UK girl punkers' mode of attire represented a rejection of all that had come before. Tight biker jackets, t-shirts ripped n' torn and acme mohair were adorned with badges, studs and day glo plastic. The Slits, in their androgynous organised mess of dressed up undress, were at the forefront of the onslaught. With righteous disregard, they smashed up the rock industry's applecart, blasting the doors open for female powerhouses to come.

In the anything-goes atmosphere of the time, other female musicians took the look in other directions. Siouxsie Sioux's fantastical approach to fashion evoked flashes of interwar Berlin decadence via Hammer Horror gore and French New Wave chic. Poly Styrene, singer of teen band X-Ray Spex, quashed '70s sexbomb clichés and expressed her femininity in an ardently individual manner: "Some people think little girls should be seen and not heard. Well I think, oh bondage, up yours."

Punk's nuclear blast was brief but devastating. Amidst the rubble, new youth culture scenes took root. Broadly termed 'post-punk', these scenes turned away from punk's decadence. Army surplus trenchcoats, V-necked jumpers and nondescript hair-dos reflected the era's somber, pseudo-industrial mood. Thatcher's reign consolidated the voices of counterculture. As Britain convulsed with societal shifts and class war, bedroom DIY labels, zines and cassette culture abounded. The Raincoats epitomised the post-punk girl look. West London art school threads married boho misshapes with mundane normality. Rhythmic, off-kilter aural excursions subtly arched against preceding rock stereotypes.

Many wimmin musicians and activists joined the forces of the anarcho punks – Situationist-inspired radicals, who merged politics with rock music in an attempt to engage public consciousness. Militaristic post-industrial chic was intended to transcend mainstream society's trivial fashion fetishes. Feminism was comfortably at home in this unisex scene with female protagonists at centre stage in bands such as Hagar the Womb, Flux of Pink Indians, Rubella Ballet and anarcho leaders, Crass.

The first all-girl indie group was Dolly Mixture. Evoking pop's mid '60s golden era, they combined car crash vignettes with middle English poetic whimsy, bridging the gap between the post-punk scene and the emergent indie underground movement.

This page: Gaye Advert,
first wave punk style icon
and lead singer of The
Adverts. London, 1977 //
Right: Pauline Murray,
Penetration, London, 1977.

12

13

14

Debsey Wykes
Guitarist, Dolly Mixture

Who inspired you to form Dolly Mixture? Were there any female musicians that compelled you to pick up an instrument?

Before we formed Dolly Mixture, Hester and I had an imaginary band called Gordon's Gay-te Crashers... I don't think it occurred to us to form a real group until we were asked to step in and sing backing vocals with a local band. They split up straight after the first gig but we had been so thrilled by the experience that we decided to get our own band together. This was early 1978, and apart from the Slits we really weren't aware of any other all-female groups and so we decided that ours would be all girls. Hester came up with the name Dolly Mixture more or less straight away. It was very much a case of trying to emulate what the boys were doing, but make it our own.

You were the first all-girl indie pop group, before indie was even a widely used term. What were the origins of the look and sound?

We had grown up with *Top of the Pops*, The Monkees and *The Partridge Family*, and had a love of pure pop and dressing up. Much of the post-punk scene was beginning to feel very dull and grey and was losing its appeal for us. We began listening to a lot more '60s music including things like the Velvet Underground... I had always been into Hollywood musicals and fashions from the '30s onwards and so I think we were absorbing all of these influences. Dr Martens and monkey boots were probably the only items of modern clothing we wore.

Where would you acquire clothes from?

As well as attending jumble sales, we gradually discovered the charity shops of Cambridge and would trawl them on a regular basis. We'd pick up anything with spots or stripes. Most of the stuff we bought wouldn't fit and so anything too small would be hung on the wall for inspiration and anything too big cut up and adapted. I still have a lot of my Dolly Mixture clothes including some wonderful Foale & Tuffin and Biba dresses that we picked up for next to nothing. We would also collect paper patterns from the '60s and make up our own outfits using either our chopped up charity shop clothes or some other cheap material.

Did you treasure a particular item of clothing back then?

I was obsessed with the black leather thigh high boots that Debbie Harry was often photographed in. One day after school a couple of friends called round and told me there was a pair my size in a nearby second hand clothes shop. They turned out to be more late '60s-looking than Debbie Harry's and unfortunately tended to concertina down my legs... but I loved them and for the for the first few months after forming the band I wore them constantly.

I first heard of Dolly Mixture from a couple of mod revival kids at school, and I assumed you were part of that scene. Were you ever considered a mod group?

In 1979, we had a fairly negative piece written about us in the *NME* saying – amongst other things – that we were riding on the coattails of the mod revival. We didn't consider ourselves to be part of any scene at all but I suppose we had a shared love of all things '60s and of course The Jam, so we did pick up a fairly strong mod following of both boys and girls. We played several shows with The Jam and were eventually signed to Paul Weller's label, so that would have reinforced any impression that we were a part of that scene.

As an all-girl group did you ever encounter any prejudice or discrimination?

Most of the boys from the bands we encountered were fairly enlightened and so we felt quite comfortable around them. However, within the extended entourage there could be some quite challenging reactions ranging from confusion to open hostility. Whenever speaking to major labels there was generally an assumption that we wouldn't be up to the task of playing on our own records and that session musicians would be required. This attitude used to infuriate us and would generally bring any talks of a possible deal to an end. If a particular label already had just one female artist on their books they usually wouldn't be interested anyway.

Can you name your top ten pre-1993 records?

This is not really our top ten pre-1993 records but these are some of the most influential records that we were all listening to when we started the band.

Singles
1. 'Shake Some Action' – Flamin' Groovies
2. 'Another Girl, Another Planet' – The Only Ones
3. 'X Offender' – Blondie
4. 'Get Over You' – Undertones
5. 'Ever Fallen In Love' – Buzzcocks

Albums
1. *Stardust* – Soundtrack Album
2. *Germ Free Adolescents* – X-Ray Spex (this was released after we formed but the singles had been very important to us)
3. *Blondie* – Blondie
4. *My Aim Is True* – Elvis Costello
5. *Ramones* – Ramones

Helen and Emma,
Wimbledon, 1980.

28

All girl post-punks the
Mo-dettes, founded by
Kate Korris of the Slits.
Birmingham, 1980.

Ana da Silva, left and
Gina Birch, right, of the
Raincoats at the Rough
Trade record shop in
Notting Hill, London, 1979.

32

This page: The Mo-dettes
play JB's in Dudley, 1981
// *Right*: Tracey Thorn on
guitar in suburban punk-
pop group, Stern Bops.
Hertford, 1980.

This page: Jane Fox of the Marine Girls sporting a '60s anorak. By the mid-'80s this was an essential indie garment. Hertford, 1982 // *Right top*: Cramps fan, Emma, Telford, 1982 // *Bottom*: Aberdeen, 1981.

This page: Early '80s Scottish indie girl style icon, Clare Grogan of Altered Images. Birmingham, 1981 // *Right*: Post-punky girl in PIL t-shirt, Telford, 1983.

USA 1977-82

We Are the One

Throughout the '70s and early '80s there was a rich back and forth cultural dialogue between London and New York. The sounds of bands including Television, Talking Heads and the Ramones, alongside female icons Patti Smith and Debbie Harry represented a return to grassroots garage rock. These bands were typically in their mid to late 20s, oozing Lower East Side boho sophistication, filtering 1960s Beat ideology through the nihilism of a city on the point of urban collapse. Their sleek, street tough, androgynous approach to fashion reverberated across the Atlantic, resounding in the consciousness of the emergent UK teen punk scene.

The UK punk scene in turn had a big impact on a budding Californian punk scene from '77 to '79. The gender inclusivity of British punk found its way into female fronted bands such as Bags, X, UXA and the Avengers. Directly influenced by the anarchic, countercultural approach of UK punk, these bands' look was a rich hodgepodge of London's King's Road via the halcyon Hollywood rock n' roll era, conjuring up William Faulkner-esque images of American Southern Gothic.

However, the California punk scene swiftly shrugged off its UK roots, taking a defiant stance into the new decade. The scene stayed young, but the people changed. From an inclusive, unisex punk idealism, the new generation was dominated by suburban, white male thrashers, taking punk into the hardcore era. Pogo dancing was replaced by slamming, the music stripped down and sped up to its bare, nihilistic bones. Women were alienated, and there were very few female musicians in this new incarnation.

Meanwhile, on the opposite coast, New York had found a new look and sound – also influenced by punk but with a more localised agenda. This was No Wave – a direct response to/rejection of New Wave rock n' roll clichés and the commercialisation of punk. A mixed bag of post-punk misfits took avant-garde art noise to its sonic extremes, incorporating the sounds of everything from free jazz to funk, punk, disco and drone rock. Although the scene was fairly male dominated, some powerful female voices could be heard. The most prominent of these was Lydia Lunch, whose confrontational performances transcended No Wave, anticipating the realms of '80s noise and death rock figureheads, Sonic Youth and the Birthday Party.

A new scene was also emerging in Washington DC. This was a more progressive, positivist punk scene centred around DIY label Dischord Records. An inclusive, mixed crowd gathered to hear hardcore bands like Minor Threat, Faith and Scream whose sound was direct, emotive and intelligent. The girls on the scene wore their hair cropped short and feathered, combining tartan skirts with American workwear/biker garb. However, these girls were mostly on the sidelines; fans rather than musicians. In fact, whilst post-punk continued its non-gendered journey in the UK, women in the US music scenes pretty much faded into invisibility.

This page: Joan Jett,
Los Angeles, 1978 //
Right: Penelope Houston
of San Francisco punk
legends, the Avengers.
Los Angeles, 1978.

This page top: Christine Sullivan and Melodye Chisholm of Phobia. Spit Club, Los Angeles, 1979 // *Bottom*: Punk girls (with Belinda Carlisle in the centre), Los Angeles, 1978 // *Right top*: LA girls, 1978 // *Bottom*: Clare Kearney and Liz Gutekunst of the Cancer Girls. Washington DC, 1979.

This page: The Bags 'We
Don't Need the English'.
Los Angeles, 1978 //
Right: Blondie 'Rip Her
to Shreds', London, 1978.

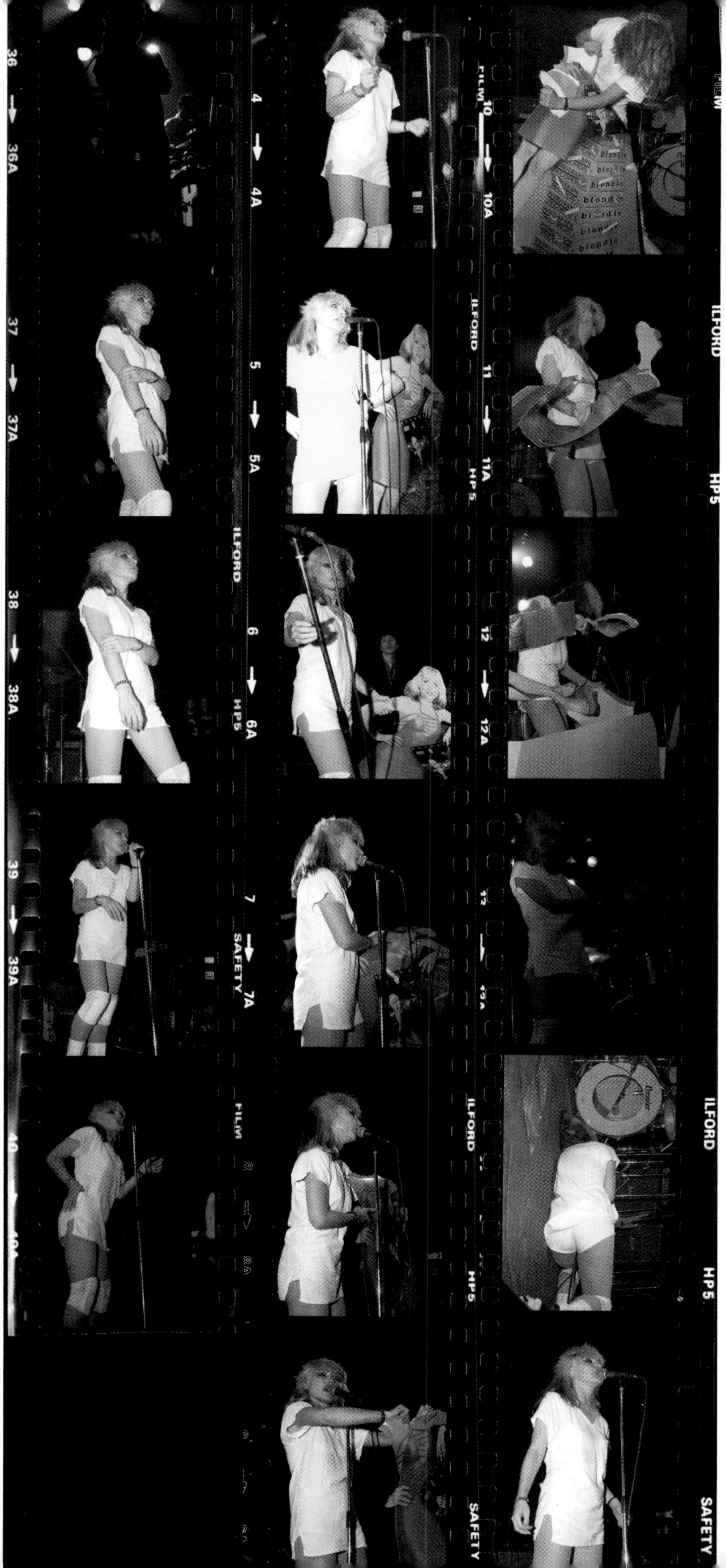
ILFORD
HP5
SAFETY
FILM

This page top: Patti Smith, Copenhagen, 1977 // *Bottom*: Kitty Moses of the X-Teens, Durham, NC, 1979 // *Right top*: Tina Weymouth, Talking Heads, New York, 1978 // *Bottom*: De De Troit of UXA supporting Black Flag. New York, 1979.

54

This page: Molly and
Nancy, Greensboro, NC,
1979 // Right: Suburban
American punk style,
Raleigh, NC, 1980.

58

This page: Poison
Ivy Rorschach of the
Cramps and friend.
Edinburgh, 1980 //
Right top and bottom:
Poison Ivy Rorschach,
Edinburgh, 1980.

60

Kira Roessler
Bass player, Black Flag

You were involved in the Hollywood punk scene early on. How did you discover it, was it love at first sight?
My older brother went to school with two of the people who eventually formed The Germs, a very early and influential LA band. I went with him to my first punk gig at The Whisky and they were playing. It was bloody and completely off the wall from what I had known. I would not say love at all. I was just going along with my brother and experiencing whatever came my way. I was generally miserable wherever I was.

Were there any particular female musicians on the scene then who inspired you to start playing bass? Who were your pet bands?
I started playing bass years before I got into punk rock. Again, the influence was my older brother. His progressive rock band lost its bass player and I decided that I would like to join. I practiced many hours a day, but was never good enough…. By the time I had any skill at all, he was into punk rock.

I played classical piano from six to 11 years old. Since I am left-handed, I always loved the bass lines in the left hand. Sometimes I wonder whether that influenced my love of bass. Of course, later I found that female bass players were around, if you paid attention.

I have always said that my influences were more the people I played with than the people I watched play. What impresses me about players is when they fit into their band perfectly, not when they stand out as exceptional.

Was there a specific punk look unique to the LA region compared to other cities in the US? What were its roots and influences?
This is hard for me to answer…. I do think that New York was potentially more influenced by New York Dolls and Patti Smith… glam, leather jackets, etc.

It always amazed me that there were these celebrity women in the LA scene purely because of their amazing look. Wild makeup, tattered fishnet stockings. They were the ones on the covers on our fanzines, and often they weren't even in bands! I mean the point was to establish something new, not imitate something else. To shock the establishment. To express non-conformity… there were no rules.

Personally, I was a tomboy and a mess. I didn't fit in with those girls who knew how to work the look… I just never cared that much about that aspect of the scene. I liked the bands and the playing.

The late '70s LA punk scene appears to have had a strong unisex balance, compared to the very masculine hardcore explosion of the '80s. Why do you think punk's evolution in the USA veered in such a macho direction, and how did it feel to be one of the few women musicians in the scene at that time?
That is very true. It seemed as if the South Bay guys poured into the gigs (as things expanded) and girls just did not. The "pogo-ing" dance moves were replaced with "slamming". Perhaps this was cause, perhaps effect. I think the anger and violence expressed in the music may have appealed more to guys. Again, I was a tomboy, so it spoke to me, but perhaps a girlie girl would feel they couldn't identify.

Kim Gordon describes you and your fashion style in the Black Flag era as being - 'one of the most startling and great things I'd seen in a long time' How would you describe your sartorial self throughout this era?

Ha! Well I had to think about that one for a while. She is totally my idol. Look, it is nothing particularly calculated. I had the clothes I had. Many were gifts and hand-me-downs. I had no money, even if I had an idea what to buy. I was completely overwhelmed just doing what I had to do: go to school, go to practice, or go on tour. It wasn't until 1985, when Henry made a comment during a photoshoot about how it would be cool if I dressed up, that it even became a thing at all. I told them if they gave me a little money I would do the whole 1985 four-month tour with a new look. I had to get help from my sister-in-law. There is no way I could have figured it out on my own. But she and I came up with the purple hair, heels and lace look, mostly because it was completely opposed to what I had been wearing until then. I had people ask if I was the same Kira. Clothes and hair are good ways to fuck with people. But I have never really felt the need to put a lot of energy into it.

When I first starting working in a corporate job, I had to figure out a uniform to try to fool people into believing I was that corporate woman. That was way harder than any other impression I ever had to make.

Did you treasure a particular item of clothing back then?

My mom had handed down this antique vest, which, was black with some gold flowers on it. It appears on a lot of old photos and I wore it until it was totally worn out. A bunch of my lace stuff was stolen out of the van on tour. I still put purple in my hair regularly.

Where would you pick clothes up from?

Before 1985, it was thrift stores or hand-me-downs. I simply had no money for clothes. When we did our special look I think we did go out and buy some lace gloves and tops. Fishnets, and maybe some black pants or a skirt too. Some heels, which I didn't have. I have no idea where. We also bought some material that I could wear as shawls to cover up if need be (the outfits were quite skimpy).

What do you feel about being regarded as a punk rock fashion icon?

That's absurd. So many people put forward powerful visual statements with their fashion. I may be a bit notorious because Black Flag is well known and I was the only female… but no I do not accept fashion icon.

What were your favourite records pre-1993?

Way to go completely off subject! I like it. Order is malleable.

1. *Meat Puppets II* – Meat Puppets
2. *Circle One* – The Germs
3. *Raw Power* – The Stooges
4. *Repeater* – Fugazi
5. *Sister* – Sonic Youth
6. *Music for Torching* – Billie Holiday
7. *Diamond Dogs* – David Bowie
8. *Nevermind* – Nirvana
9. *Saint Vitus* – Saint Vitus

Julia Gorton in a motel,
New York, 1979.

This page top: The Island, Houston, 1981 // *Bottom*: The Disposals, Los Angeles, 1979 // *Right top*: Texas femme art punks, Mydolls, who later featured in Wim Wenders' 1984 cult film, *Paris Texas*. Houston, 1981 // *Bottom*: Indie record store new wave fashions. Houston, 1980.

This page: Angela Jaeger, singer of Stare Kits in vintage Western styling. New York, 1979 // *Right clockwise from top left*: Linda Ramone, New York, 1978; Vintage/New Wave, Oakland, 1981; Monica Richard in Harrington jacket and brooches, Washington DC, 1981; Youth punk scene, Los Angeles, 1981.

This page: Exene Cervenka of X, Los Angeles, 1981 // *Right top*: DC punk youth, Christine Steele, Washington DC, 1982 // *Bottom*: Death rocker Misfits fan, San Francisco, 1982.

This page: DC hardcore punk style — a cool, tough, uniquely East Coast urban amalgamation of UK skinhead via US hardcore nihilisims. Washington DC, 1981 // *Right*: Christine Steele — DC HC. Washington DC, 1982.

The Wrecks, all-girl Reno
teen punk rock thrashers.
Reno NV, 1981.

80

Before they became the Bangles, the Bangs were Paisley Underground pop sensations. Los Angeles, 1982.

UK 1983-87

A Scene
in
Between

As the post-punk scene began to wind down, a new British youth scene bubbled to the surface; indie. With unemployment at record-breaking heights and Thatcherism in full swing, pockets of young people fell into a subdued survival state of peaceful protest and escapism as a means of creative expression. The sheer rage of punk proved to be unsustainable, and by the early to mid '80s it was spent. With student and dole culture as a backdrop, indie offered an intellectual retreat from reality and from gaudy, synthetic mainstream society.

This scene looked towards specific aspects of the mid-'60s and late-'70s for sonic and sartorial inspiration. Bands like Subway Sect and Television Personalities merged the minor key janglings of sub-Byrds garage bands circa '65/'66 with '60s Shangri La girl group urban dramas and the art school end of punk to create something entirely new. Savvier and more switched on than previous scenes, the indie scene was completely inclusive and unisex. The Pastels, Shop Assistants, Jesse Garon, Talulah Gosh, Vaselines and My Bloody Valentine were all of balanced gender makeup.

The women in these bands often dressed the same as the boys; The Velvet Underground's legacy loomed large. Velvet's drummer, Moe Tucker, was a big fashion icon – black shades, rollnecks and leather trousers were paired with droning, tinny feedbacking guitars played in a stoically detached pose. Other girls went for a more Marine Girls fashion approach; abstract '50s and early '60s print dresses were worn with twinset cardies, for a nursery-rhymes/Ladybird book innocence that was offset by Dr Martens or monkey boots.

The cassette/DIY/zine culture continued to operate as an underground network, bringing together like-minded youth around the country. Through it, there was a revival of interest in 1960s American underground music. Reissues and bootleg compilations brought these nuggets back from the grave, and *Texas Flashbacks* were de rigueur alongside contemporary UK releases in any indie kid's record collection. However, initially there was very little way of accessing contemporary American indie subculture; the UK scene was largely isolated in its localised bubble. Towards the middle of the '80s, a handful of fanzines began to appear and a few independent record shops began to specialise in small label imports. Gradually, international reverberations began to be felt, and rare visits from Stateside brethren Sonic Youth, Pussy Galore and Beat Happening cracked through the insularity. By '88/'89 the exploding US scene could not help but garner the interest of British indie youth and things began to open up.

This page top: Gina Davidson of the Marine Girls, Margate, 1983 // *Bottom*: Indie-mod crossover girl, Newquay, 1985 // *Right top*: Gina Davidson in Enid Blyton *Famous Five* styling. London, 1983 // *Bottom*: London mod militia, 1985.

Gina Davidson
Marine Girls

To be truthful I don't think I was aware of fashion until the early '80s. Like most kids I had favourite items like my Marc Bolan tee and a pair of hand-me-down hotpants from my cousin. Later, I loved clothes and having my own style… but I don't think the idea of fashion hit me until I started buying *ID* and *The Face* and then I got into brands and buying clothes from young designers at Kensington Market. The answer to this then must be music.....

I think I first became aware of the existence of punk by seeing a girl in the sixth form in the dinner queue at school wearing one feather in one ear and two piercings in the other. RADICAL. I investigated further and started to buy the *NME* and listen to John Peel. My local record shop was really great and had all the new Rough Trade releases and some bootleg LP's on the back wall. Through that shop I connected to musically-minded people in my local town, and that is how I met Mark Flunder.

Prior to Marine Girls, what bands were you going to see play live or listening to records by?

I didn't see that many live bands prior to Marine Girls as we lived in the middle of nowhere and I was totally reliant on my parents driving me anywhere.... I was listening to the Buzzcocks, Clash, Siouxsie and the Banshees, Adam and the Antz, Penetration, Durutti Column, Swell Maps, the Slits, the Raincoats, the Jam, The Fall, Television Personalities, Teenage Filmstars, O'Level, Cult Figures, Big in Japan, Pink Military, Joy Division....

Were there particular female musicians that inspired you to form a band?

Yes, the Raincoats (they seemed like us but MUCH older!) the Slits, Poly Styrene, Pauline Murray, Lesley woods from the Au Pairs, Alison Statton of Young Marble Giants.

Growing up in the suburban Home Counties in the pre-internet age, how did you discover the underground scene and connect with like-minded individuals?

A lot of my discoveries were due to Nikki Sudden from Swell Maps. I was a huge fan and wrote to him at the address on the back of their single. He replied and was very helpful, putting me in touch with other people that wrote to him.... He worked at Rough Trade and I would go and hang out there… Quite often bands would put their addresses on the back of their singles / cassettes / zines. Later, me and Jane and Tracey did our own zine.

I made an awful lot of friends via Paul Platypus (Rosen) from Twelve Cubic Feet who had also written to Nikki. There was a little web of people all interconnected. Dan Treacy lived in the next flat to Alan McGee, so we had the Creation connection with The Pastels. There was a LOT of letter writing and compilation tape swaps. It all seemed quite natural…. It's a bit of a blur now, like a homogeneous mass of interconnected people..... Of course it was also about playing and going to gigs put on by the people that wrote the zines.

The Marine Girls' distinctive look eventually became became an indie girl template. Can you describe the influences behind the look?

Part of the inspiration for me came from my childhood clothes: anoraks with pretty binding, t-bar shoes and Clarks sandals, cotton summer dresses and suede jackets. A bit *Famous Five*. The things that we liked were easy to find in charity shops and at jumble sales and we didn't have a lot of money to spend.

Also, I suppose being at school together and spending a lot of time in each other's company we developed a look. I remember a cotton '50s skirt that I adapted with cross over straps that looked like it was straight out of a learn-to-read book from nursery school. We took our jeans in, as you couldn't buy tight straight-legged jeans, and wore them with striped t-shirts and black elasticated school PE shoes, duffle coats and pixie boots.... The only new things I bought were the occasional pair of shoes from Kensington Market.

Post-punk was a very gender inclusive scene. Do you think this was already changing by the early '80s? As an all-girl group did you confront any discrimination?

I don't think it really crossed my mind. We were just all so wrapped up in making music. I mean obviously we were aware of being in an all-female group, but that didn't seem important at the time. We did have a few hecklers at our gigs – I think they were just trying to provoke a reaction and see what we would do.... There was some level of condescension, but I think that was more a case of not being the traditional band set up and playing a type of music that sounded amateurish and different.

Beach Party is widely revered as an indie DIY classic. How does feel to be part of something so seminal?

It feels very special. I'm so proud of what we did. It felt amazing and different at the time and I still think that it feels that way today.

Can you list your top ten favourite records from pre-1993?

1. *Rum Sodomy and the Lash / Red Roses For Me* – The Pogues
2. *The Scream* – Siouxsie and the Banshees
3. *A Trip To Marineville* – Swell Maps
4. *You Can't Hide Your Love Forever* – Orange Juice
5. *Dare* – Human League
6. *Steve McQueen* – Prefab Sprout
7. *D.O.A: The Third And Final Report* – Throbbing Gristle
8. *And Don't The Kids Just Love It* – Television Personalities
9. *Colossal Youth* – Young Marble Giants
10. *The Return Of The Durutti Column* – The Durutti Column

This page top: Annabel (Aggi) Wright of The Pastels, in '60s art school threads. Bearsden, 1985 // Bottom: Karen with Vox Phantom. Glasgow, 1985 // Right top: Shop Assistants, Glasgow, 1985 // Bottom: Tracy of the Primitives, London, 1986.

This page: Talulah Goshers, Glasgow, 1987 // *Right top*: Bridget Duffy of the Sea Urchins — Sarah Records 001 seminal coolness. London, 1987 // *Bottom*: Birmingham indie girls, 1987.

Mid-'80s mod goddess Fay
Hallam of Makin Time at the
100 Club, London, 1985.

This page top: Jo, Telford,
1983 // Bottom: London,
1984 // Right top: Primal
Scream fan, Brighton,
1987 // Bottom: Skinnipin,
Arbroath, 1984.

Indie record store assistant.
Canterbury, 1985.

This page top: Sue, Telford, 1985 // Bottom: Annabel (Aggi) Wright of The Pastels. Bearsden, 1988 // Right top: Rover Girls at the Hammersmith Clarendon, London, 1986 // Bottom: 'We've got a Fuzzbox and we're going to use it'. London, 1986.

This page: Laurel sporting
some Velvets-inspired
Creation Records chic.
London, 1987 // *Right*:
Elvina Flower of London
noisenics the Sperm Wails,
Metro Club, London, 1987.

JESUS AND MARY CHAIN

DARKLANDS

The Ca

OUT

LEAR COMPACT CAS

TO DO

CD · LP · CA

Brighton Dome
Sunday
27th September
The Mint Juleps
Attacco Decente
Hank Wangford
PLUS SPECIAL GUESTS
A BENEFIT
CONCERT FOR
ANTI APARTHEID
Tickets: £5
Doors: 7.30pm

Brighton Dome
Sunday
27th September
The Mint Juleps
Attacco Decente
Hank Wangford
PLUS SPECIAL GUESTS
A BENEFIT
CONCERT FOR
ANTI APARTHEID
Tickets: £5
Doors: 7.3

Brighton
Sunday
27th Sep
The M
Attacco
Hank

This page top: Bridget
Duffy of the Sea Urchins,
Birmingham, 1986 // *Bottom*:
Indie girl, London, 1983 //
Right: Fashion student
Vicki Poole, Southend, 1986.

110

This page top: Bex of Loop.
Croydon, 1986 // *Bottom*:
Indie pop unknowns, the
Hobgoblins. London, 1987.
// *Right top*: Bilinda of
My Bloody Valentine,
Portlands, London, 1987.
// *Bottom*: Alison Pate and
Jo Wiggs of Perfect Disaster
with the photographer, Heidi
Schramli. London, 1987.

112

Donna Kebab, drummer.
Brighton, 1988.

116

USA 1983-87

Expressway
to
Yr. Skull

By 1983, the US indie music scenes were virtually devoid of female musicians. Even in progressive punk scenes, women were seen but not heard. A few minor girl bands, such as Frightwig and Chalk Circle, tried to break through, but none managed to capture a wider flight of imagination.

In 1985, a group of DC scenesters came together to take a stand against the senseless violence and machismo of hardcore and US punk. Challenging the aggression of slamdancing and the undercurrent of sexism throughout the scenes, a long hot season of discussion and debate ensued. This became known as Revolution Summer and it spawned Positive Force, an activist collective that sought radical social change for women within the punk scene and beyond. Revolution Summer is perceived as the spiritual birthplace of riot grrrl, which emerged five years later.

Without a doubt, the trailblazer of this era was Sonic Youth. Exploring rock's outer limits via controlled feedback, their droneout noise jams were capable of levelling entire city blocks, and yet they managed to retain the guise of a classical four-piece rock outfit. As a New York band, they very clearly carried the legacy of No Wave, whilst also anticipating the noise rock scene to come. Bass player Kim Gordon was a new brand of female musician, whose art school, bohemian image created a template for all who followed. Standing in a pose of stoic reserve as the boys sent their guitars into interstellar overdrive, she anchored the band, saving it from terminal male guitar geekdom and infusing it with her effortless cool.

Simultaneous to Sonic Youth's ascent, a new scene was emerging in the bohemian enclave of Olympia, Washington. This scene revolved around the band Beat Happening and their label, K Records. Comprised of Calvin Johnson, Bret Haris and Heather Lewis, Beat Happening's sound was a meeting of UK ramshackle indie pop a la Marine Girls via a Cramps-like bassless garage thud. The band took a rotating group structure with Heather and Calvin taking turns on vocal duties. In 1988, Beat Happening toured the UK with Glasgow indie iconoclasts, the Vaselines, creating a natural transatlantic link between the indie capitals of Olympia and Glasgow. The dots were slowly being joined together.

Fashion-wise, the indie rock scenes on both the East and West coasts took a similar approach. Thrift store college Ts and sweats were worn with sneakers and washed out plaid or Oxford shirts. This shabby, preppy look might now seem understated to the point of mundane, but when viewed in context, it offered a subversive counterbalance to flashy, mainstream MTV-dominated music culture.

In spite of a few high profile women on bass or drums, the scenes continued to be very male dominated well into the late '80s. Whilst the third wave of feminism was bubbling away in discussion groups and college dorms, it wasn't finding expression on the music scene. Yet.

This page top and bottom:
DC crowds, 1983 // *Right
top*: Erica Hoffman's
suburban bedroom. DC, 1985
// *Bottom*: Sarah Borruso of
SF peace punks, Atrocity.
San Francisco, 1984.

124

This page top: Berkeley
preppy mod girl, 1987
// *Bottom*: Paisley
Undergrounders the
Pandoras, Los Angeles,
1983 // *Right*: Patricia
Morrison of The Gun Club,
Los Angeles, 1983.

126

This page: Linda LeSabre, DC, 1983 // *Right*: Madhouse, DC, 1983.

DC youth scene, 1983.

This page top: Lara Lynch, singer of noise punk outfit Nuclear Crayons, DC, 1983 // *Bottom*: Paisley Undergrounder, San Francisco, 1986 // *Right top and bottom*: Seattle, 1983.

Berkeley peace punx
scenesters, 1984.

Danceteria night club,
New York, 1985.

This page top: Salem 66,
Connecticut, 1985 //
Bottom: Myra Power, DC,
1986 // Right: The youth
of Revolution Summer.
DC, 1985.

142

Seminal garage punk noise,
Julie Cafritz, Pussy
Galore. New Jersey, 1987.

Julie Cafritz
Guitarist, Pussy Galore

When did you first become interested in music and fashion?

Growing up, I found myself tortured by the guitar heroes of my older brothers: Jimi Hendrix, Jeff Beck, Duane Allman, Clapton. You name them, I hated them. HATED THEM. I would become physically ill. My stomach hurt at the sound of a guitar solo.... The only rock band I liked was the Rolling Stones. Mick and Keith (with either Marianne or Anita, and later Bianca on their arms) reminded me of my own very glamorous and decadent brothers and their freaky, fabulous friends and girlfriends. I think it was much later that I realised that it was my brothers who were copying the Stones and not the other way around. I was captivated by the fur vests, the unbuttoned shirts with leather necklaces and the eye makeup. That effortless hodge-podge hippie chic, coupled with the fact that for the most part, the Stones did not indulge in wanky guitar solos, gave them the pass that I did not allow any other rock band.

Who influenced you to become a musician, what bands/artists were you into when you were growing up?

Besides a seasonal detour into reggae music, prompted by yearly visits to Jamaica starting in 1970, I didn't really listen to music until I started listening to black radio stations in the mid-'70s. Then I fell in love with Earth, Wind and Fire, the Isley Brothers, the Whispers, the Brothers Johnson, Stevie Wonder, Le Chic, the Gap Band. Ohio Players, Heat Wave... I could go on but you get the picture. This was happy music, full of love and positivity and as disco took over, the sound of the guitar became less abrasive and was eventually replaced by synthesisers. I loved disco.

The production on those records, contrary to popular belief, was amazing. So as the '70s became the '80s, my ears were primed for New Wave and I fell hard.

How would describe your fashion image throughout the '80s and early '90s?

Fashion-wise, I arrived at college in 1983 as a cross between Jennifer Beals and Madonna, having just recently shed my preppy uniform. And now that I have revealed that, I must kill you. First my music taste began to morph; it was a hop skip and jump from Thomas Dolby and Echo and the Bunnymen to Fad Gadget and New Order.... I started to fall into a depression, and so naturally, I started to get into Goth music, which led me to a more Gothy sense of style.... Eventually I died my hair blue/black and started teasing it. I dropped out of college and started working at a vintage clothing store.... The Madonna rubber bracelets remained a constant but everything else changed.

I shopped almost exclusively at thrift stores, even when I moved away from Goth into proto-grunge wear at the end of the '80s. Once I was in bands, I could scour the world looking for cool, one-of-a kind, ringer tees and Levi's 517 cords. I embraced colour big time. My sister, Daisy, was a stylist so I really just followed her style lead....

Were there female music icons you related to, or aspired to emulate as a youth?

I am perhaps different than many others who found themselves in bands because my position was that I hated music and didn't play an instrument but I still thought I could start a better band than the shitty bands my friends (all male) were in. It was a position founded out of sheer bravado and in pure ignorance. I wasn't emulating anyone, female or male, because I had no heroes or role models. I knew what I didn't want it to sound like rather than what I did. Jon and I spoke about it sounding like a garage band meets an industrial band, which I liked the idea of, but it was all rather abstract and intellectual for me, rather than motivated by passion.

The US '80s indie rock, punk scenes appeared to be very male heavy, why do think it was so unbalanced?
Rock was by definition cock-oriented. When I started Pussy Galore in 1985, there just weren't any girls in bands that I knew of, with the exception of Kim Gordon and Jarboe and Brix. For me being a girl was the least of my barriers, see previous answer relating to hating music and not playing an instrument. If you had to be as blithe as I was, it is frankly not that surprising there weren't more girls in bands.

Your time with Pussy Galore pre-dates the riot grrrl scene by a few years, did you imagine at the time you were paving the way for the next wave of female musicians?
Not really. Girls were constantly coming up to me and telling me that I was really inspiring, but I took it with a grain of salt, like the kid in the wheelchair who finishes the marathon, getting a ribbon just for reaching the finish line. I thought I wore my incompetence and disdain on my sleeve so I shook off what I thought were just idle compliments.

When riot grrrl came along, there was an interest in cataloguing and writing their history from the outset. And I remember being really struck by how knowledgeable they were. Even though STP had

really lasted all of nine months, so many riot grrrls in the US had managed to see a date on our one big tour (opening for Sonic Youth and Nirvana). In the UK, they had managed to get their hands on our one 7". Unlike me, they had taken a deep dive into history, had role models and were starting bands with a real purpose. Most of them were not nearly as familiar with Pussy Galore as they were with STP and Free Kitten and I found myself sort of as an honorary elder statesman, which of course was genuinely flattering.

Can you list your favourite records from pre-1993?

1. *This Nation's Saving Grace, Hex Enduction Hour, Perverted by Language, Room to Live* and all The Fall EPs of that period.
2. *Hole and Nail* – Scraping Foetus off the Wheel
3. *Long Arm of the Lord* – Cabaret Voltaire
4. *Locust Abortion Technicians* – Butthole Surfers
5. *Atomizer, Hammer Party, Songs About Fucking* – Big Black

This page: Lydia Lunch,
London, 1987 // *Right*: Julie
Cafritz of Pussy Galore,
The Rat, Boston, 1987.

150

152

This page top: Street
punks, Boston, 1985 //
Bottom: Bored indie
girl. Lawrence KS, 1986.
Right: Kim Gordon,
Connecticut, 1987.

Husker Du fan, New
Jersey, 1984.

UK 1988-93

Our Troubled Youth

By 1988, the UK indie scene was evolving out of the fuzzy, Velvety jingle jangle of the Pastels, Jesus and Mary Chain and Primal Scream, into the new territory of shoegaze. This scene took inspiration from the lysergic sounds of '60s acid punk compilations and the drone elements of the debut Stooges, 13th Floor Elevators and second Velvets LPs. Contemporary US indie racketeers Dinosaur Jr and Sonic Youth were also influential.

Bands such as Spacemen 3 would sit on chairs staring at their instruments or the floor, ignoring the crowd in a semi-detached state of psychedelic solitude. Some went so far as to turn their backs to the audience. It was a downbeat, self-deprecating scene – introverted with little ego or machismo. Bands such as Slowdive, Telescopes, Curve, My Bloody Valentine and Lush had a mixed gender makeup; ethereal female vocals would barely break through the symphonic din of distortion pedals and repetitive hypnotic riffs.

The shoegaze look was a scruffier version of indie; longer hair, baggy jumpers, more anti-fashion. Bilinda Butcher of My Bloody Valentine was an archetypal shoegaze scene girl. Cool, detached and androgynous, she wore Kim Gordon-esque boho mashups with hints of mod/goth (moth) leanings.

Shoegaze was often panned in press circles for existing in a cave state of insularity and some indie pop kid purists turned towards Bristol's Sarah Records for continuing submersion into the whimsical anorak-clad netherworld of jangle. Sarah Records sounded slightly out of time, referencing a scene that had only just passed. Bands such as the Field Mice and Heavenly bravely weathered the storm, releasing slews of 45s that harked back to early Creation and Postcard's jangliest pop moments. Proudly DIY in its aesthetic, the label became almost a sub-genre in its own right, achieving worldwide mythical status.

In the meantime, the introduction of ecstasy was having a cataclysmic effect on British youth scenery. The rise of E and acid house created an unbreachable schism between the progressive pilled-up ravers in the clubs and the shoegazing daydreamers in the pubs. Each was revelling in their own form of escapism from late '80s reality. 'Drugs not jobs' was a slogan that effectively encompassed the head-in-the-sand youth culture.

In '91, Brighton's Huggy Bear responded to the Stateside tremors emanating from the DC and Olympia scenes, chanelling the American preppy-mod look and mixing it up with a bit of C86 ancestry. Sharing a split LP with Bikini Kill entitled *Our Troubled Youth*, Huggy Bear was the UK representative of the riot grrrl wave that was sweeping the US.

Skinned Teen was another rare UK adopter of the riot grrrl politics and primitive punk assault of the DC/Olympia scenes. A genuine teen punk girl band, they, along with Huggy Bear, represented a brief return to true DIY youth culture during the slow fade of early '90s UK indie scenery.

This page top: Student digs, London, 1989 // *Bottom*: Alisonwonderland and Delia at Rough Trade, London, 1990 // Right: Indie student, London, 1989.

This page: Shoegazer in Leeds, 1991 // Right top: Huggy Bear, Bradford, 1992 // Bottom: Slowdive, Bristol, 1991.

This page top: Liverpool, 1989 // *Bottom*: Katie Pugsley of Pooh Sticks, London, 1989 // *Right top*: Leatitia Sadier of McCarthy, Barking, 1989 // *Bottom*: Jo Doran of The Telescopes in Velvets-inspired garms. London, 1989.

172

This page: Anne Mari Davies from Sarah Records janglers, The Field Mice. Bristol, 1990 // *Right:* Silverfish play the Dome, London, 1991.

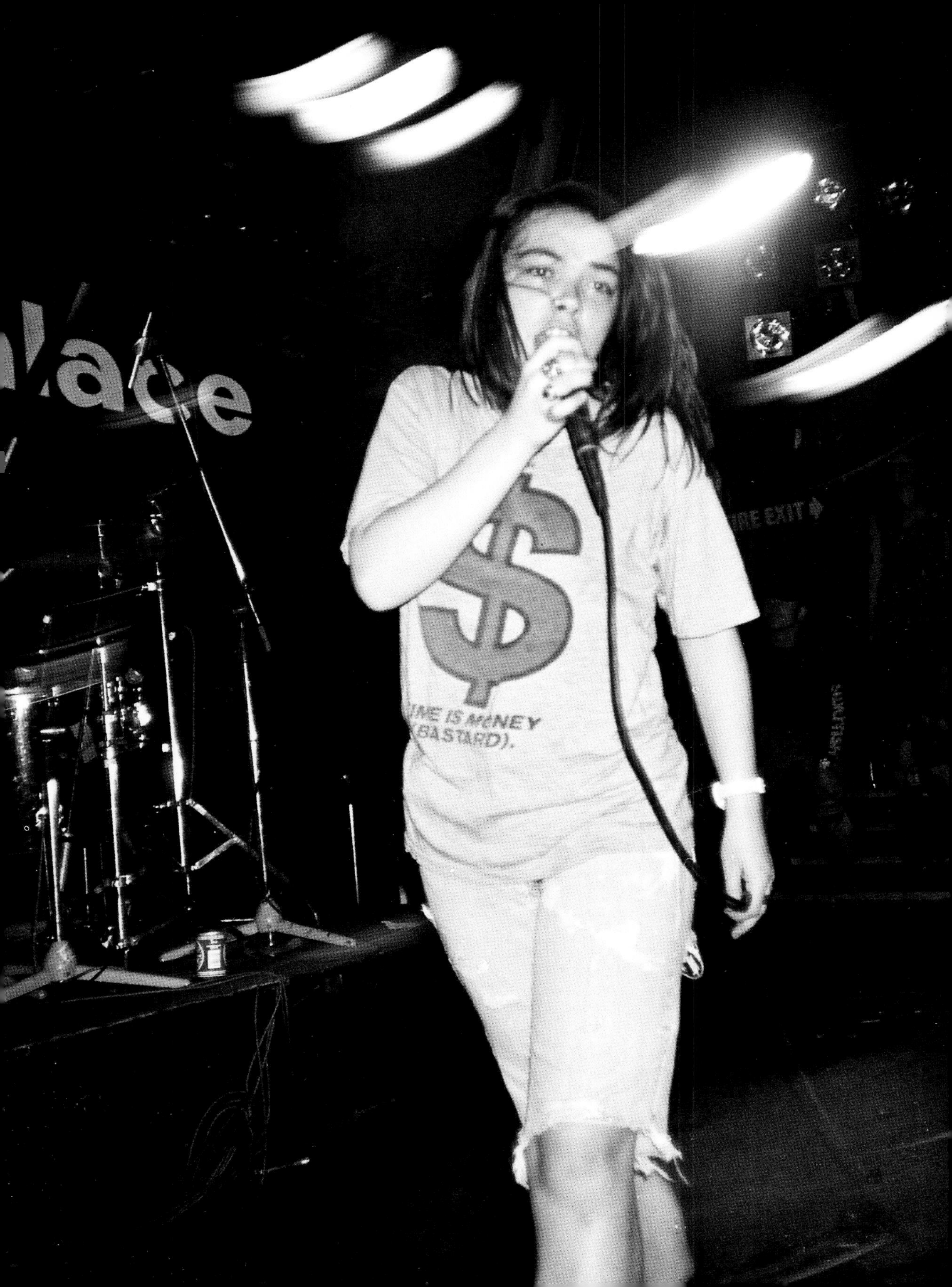

lace
IME IS MONEY
(BASTARD).
IRE EXIT

This page top: Brighton
student bedroom, 1991 //
Bottom: Melody Dog, Glasgow,
1991 // *Right top*: Pat of
Melody Dog, Glasgow, 1991
// *Bottom*: Lindsay,
Yorkshire, 1989.

PJ Harvey, London, 1991.

Bilinda Butcher, London, 1989.

This page top: Jo Johnson of Huggy Bear, Leicester, 1992 // Bottom: Jo Johnson, London, 1992 // Right: Huggy Bear, London, 1992.

Amelia Fletcher, Heavenly,
London, 1993.

Skinned Teen, London, 1993.

190

USA 1988-93

Revolution Girl
Style Now

In 1988, Olympia-based writer, Tobi Vale, wrote an article called 'Boxes' in her seminal zine, *Jigsaw*. In it she discussed gender issues within the punk scenes. The article was read by local student, Kathleen Hanna, who made contact with Vail and the two started a new zine and a rock group, both entitled Bikini Kill. *Jigsaw* was also an inspiration for young student feminists Molly Neuman and Allison Wolfe, who likewise started a fanzine called *Girl Germs* and a band called Bratmobile. After a decade of silence, women were finally rising up to confront sexism and homophobia and reclaim the domain of punk. The youth wave explosion called riot grrrl had begun.

Riot grrrl groups played stripped down garage punk in the vein of Beat Happening, early Slits and the Shaggs. Sartorially, everything from UK indie, preppy mod, '60s suburban dork chic and post-punk's misshapes were put through the fashion blender, and reimagined for the grrrl generation.

In 1991, Calvin Johnson of Beat Happening organised the International Pop Underground Convention (IPU) in Olympia. The opening night of this six-day festival was entitled Love Rock Revolution Girl Style Now. Its all-female lineup included Bikini Kill, Bratmobile, Heavens to Betsy, 7 Year Bitch and others. Later simply referred to as 'Girl Night', it became the stuff of legends for riot grrrls worldwide.

Around this period, a new underground scene was beginning to materialise in Seattle. Known as 'grunge', it pushed post hardcore/college rock meanderings into a new sound that combined crud punk with suburban stoner riffage. From '89 onwards, bands such as Mudhoney, Tad, Melvins and Nirvana embodied an unpretentious, down home, grassroots look and sound that celebrated their provincial, high school loser status. The scene was unisex in its makeup; Hole and White Zombie were mixed bands, whilst Babes In Toyland, L7, STP and Lunachicks had all-girl lineups. The girls often wore the same apathetic mess of unkempt androgyny as the guys. Others opted for Baby Jane dresses from the '40s and '50s with heavy duty engineer boots and plaid trucker shirts evoking the halcyon era of American industrial greatness. Hair was worn long and shapeless in response to the cropped heads of hardcore and the backcombed fantasy of metal.

The overnight success of Nirvana changed everything and the scene pretty much ate itself as major labels flocked to the city to sign up anything remotely grunge. It was punk all over again.

Two decades later it's becoming possible to assess the legacy of the riot grrrl phenomenon, the final piece in the punk jigsaw. By taking ownership of a massively male-dominated punk scene, riot grrrl opened the door for generations of women's voices to be heard. The ideals of social change through DIY punk rock have been carried forward by numerous girl bands today. The story of women in independent music is one that will continue to unfold as Untypical Girls of the future keep the revolutionary spirit alive.

This page: White Zombie, Boston, 1988 // *Right*: Tobi Vail and Kathleen Hanna of Bikini Kill at Rock For Choice. DC, 1992.

This page top: Heather Lewis of Beat Happening whilst on tour with the Vaselines. Loch Lomond, Scotland, 1988 // Bottom: Boston, 1988 // Right top and bottom: Cult feminist punks, Frightwig, San Francisco, 1989.

200

This page: San Francisco, 1991 // *Right*: Wendy, Ohio, 1989.

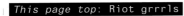

This page top: Riot grrrls at the March for Women's Lives, DC, 1992 // *Bottom*: Slant 6 at the Embassy, DC, 1992 // *Right*: Riot grrrls, DC, 1992.

208

210

This page top: Carrie Brownstein, Excuse 17, DC, 1993 // *Bottom*: Bratmobile, DC, 1993 // *Right top*: Jenny Toomey and Kristin Thomson in the Simple Machines office, Arlington VA, 1991 // *Bottom*: 'The Future is Female', DC, 1991.

214

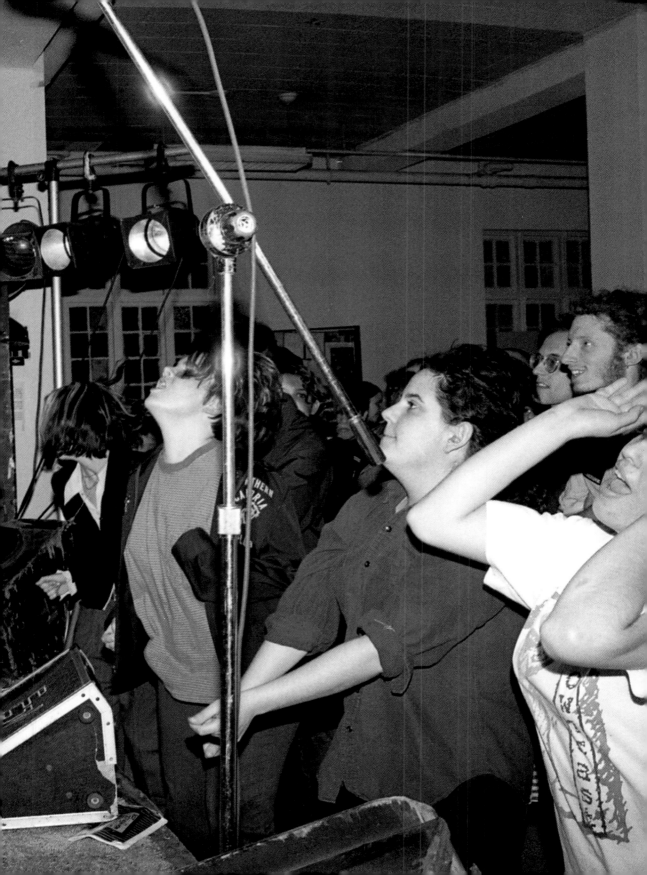

220

222

This page top and right:
Rebel Girl tattoos inspired
by the Bikini Kill song.
DC, 1992 // Bottom: Riot
grrrls at the March for
Women's Lives, DC, 1992.

224

226

This page: Kathy Wilcox of Bikini Kill, Olympia, 1991 // *Right top*: Rachael McNally of Sleepyhead loading up the tour van. New Jersey, 1991 // *Bottom*: Bratmobile at IPU.

Erin Smith
Guitarist, Bratmobile

How did you discover music when you were growing up?

I grew up in the Washington DC suburbs in Bethesda, Maryland. There was an amazing underground scene. From the age of 11, I shopped at an incredible record store called Yesterday & Today Records in Rockville, Maryland, where I got all of my records. Two of the main record store clerks there were Guy Picciotto and Brendan Canty, then of Rites of Spring, later of Fugazi. They were incredibly patient and kind, getting rare 7"s off of the wall and keeping special reserved copies behind the counter for me.... I wouldn't be who I am today without Yesterday & Today!.... I also wrote away for catalogues and rarities from *Goldmine,* a magazine for record collectors. I got several record collecting pen pals through that and shared knowledge that way.

What bands and types of music were you into in your youth?

I was a complete super fan of whatever I was in to, so only ever liked one band at a time, but liked them completely obsessively. First it was Duran Duran. In 1984, I fully immersed myself in finding out all I could about the UK New Romantic scene.... That didn't go over well in the halls of my junior high. Then it was Depeche Mode, then a full on obsession with The Smiths, collecting every last 7". I loved all kinds of UK underground from there – often things that I read Morrissey was into. I only read UK teen magazines, which weren't hard to find due to all of the UK expats in DC. After that I got into Beat Happening, the whole Olympia/K Records scene, and then the local DC/Dischord scene. I still have a special fondness for C86 and British twee pop.

Who inspired you to become a musician? Were there any particular female musicians that compelled you to pick up an instrument?

I thought I would never be "good enough" to be in a band until I got into the K Records DIY scene, when I realised anyone could do it.

I was super influenced by Heather Lewis of Beat Happening and Tobi Vail when she was in the Go Team (pre-Bikini Kill), and really influenced by Calvin Johnson and Billy Karren as well. I loved Kim Deal, Kim Gordon, and Julia Cafritz as well as DC's own Autoclave (Christina Billotte and Mary Timony). I remember staring at Headcoatees' records and just really, really wanting to be in an all-girl band. It was actually Jeff McDonald of Redd Kross that in the late '80s told me to stop being shy and write original songs. I listened to his advice and bought my first guitar from my brother's housemate, Mike Schulman, who was in Black Tambourine at the time... It was covered in Black Tambourine graffiti and remained my main guitar throughout the entirety of Bratmobile.

Very early on, while still in high school I played a show with Lois of K Records under the name Bobby Sox Bandit Queens, then began jamming with Christina and Mira Billotte, who I'd gone to elementary school with.

When I eventually joined Bratmobile, I was incredibly lucky to have such amazing friends who were also musicians. I can't stress enough how powerful it was to have the support of female musicians who I also admired greatly, like Tobi Vail, Kathleen Hanna and Kathi Wilcox from Bikini Kill, Corin Tucker and Tracy Sawyer from Heavens to Betsy and Amelia Fletcher from Heavenly. I couldn't have asked for greater ladies to play with and learn from!

The early first wave riot grrrl fashion look was a radical DIY mish mash of previous music / fashion subcultures, can you describe where these elements derived from? And like punk beforehand, did it eventually become a fashion uniform?

On the grounds that riot grrrl was too often pigeon-holed as a fashion-centered movement rather than a musical or feminist one, I shouldn't answer this. I will say I was way more into the tights, cut off shorts, and thrift store T-shirts of the stereotypical riot grrrl look than the baby doll dresses and barrettes! I think unfortunately the fashion began to overshadow the real meaning of the movement, at least in some of the mainstream press.

What were your sartorial inspirations during the early '90s and where would you pick clothes up from?

I don't think there was anyone in the DC punk scene of the early '90s that wasn't influenced by the fashions of Nation of Ulysses. They were one of the most perfect looking bands ever and were much copied. Wearing all black, vintage auto club jackets, dyed black hair, etc... Pure perfection! There were lots of vintage clothing stores in DC back in the day. I got most of my clothes at vintage shops, thrift stores, and estate sales.

I remember seeing Bratmobile play at the Chameleon Club, San-Francisco and it felt like I was actually witnessing a female youth punk rock revolution. How did it feel to be in the thick of a historically vital feminist wave movement?

The Chameleon San Francisco show was in June, 1992 on our first US tour. It was amazing to be in the middle of it, but at the time I thought why do anything at all if you're not going to do something huge? A lot of people who were there at the time will say they never knew it would become anything or have lasting influence. I always knew and always felt it would.

What were your top ten favourite records pre-1993?

I'm not including mix tapes here, which I listened to constantly, or the pre-1993 demo tapes of my close friends and peers like Heavens To Betsy, Bikini Kill, and Autoclave. Impossible to keep it to just ten!

1. *Hatful of Hollow, The Queen is Dead* – The Smiths
2. *Beat Happening, Jamboree* – Beat Happening
3. *Psychocandy* – The Jesus & Mary Chain
4. *Up for a Bit* – The Pastels
5. *Ecstasy and Wine, Isn't Anything* – My Bloody Valentine
6. *Surfer Rosa* – Pixies
7. *Daydream Nation, Goo* – Sonic Youth
8. *Duran Duran, Rio* – Duran Duran
9. *Leisure* – Blur
10. *Imperial f.f.r.r., Perfect Teeth* – Unrest
11. *Heavenly vs. Satan, Le Jardin De Heavenly* – Heavenly

This page: Slant 6, DC, 1993 // *Right top*: Feminist grunge rockers, L7, play the Rock for Choice benefit. DC, 1992 // *Bottom*: Tiger Trap, DC, 1992.

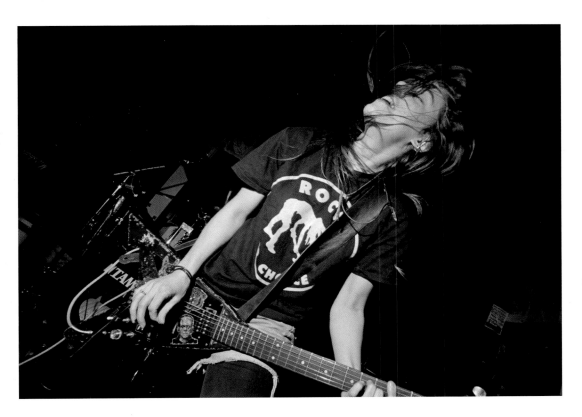

This page top: Roxanne and Lala, (Lara Allen of Broome and Caroliner), 1991 // *Bottom*: Trailer queens, Portland, 1992 // *Right*: Mamie Lane at the Chameleon Club, San Francisco, 1991.

240

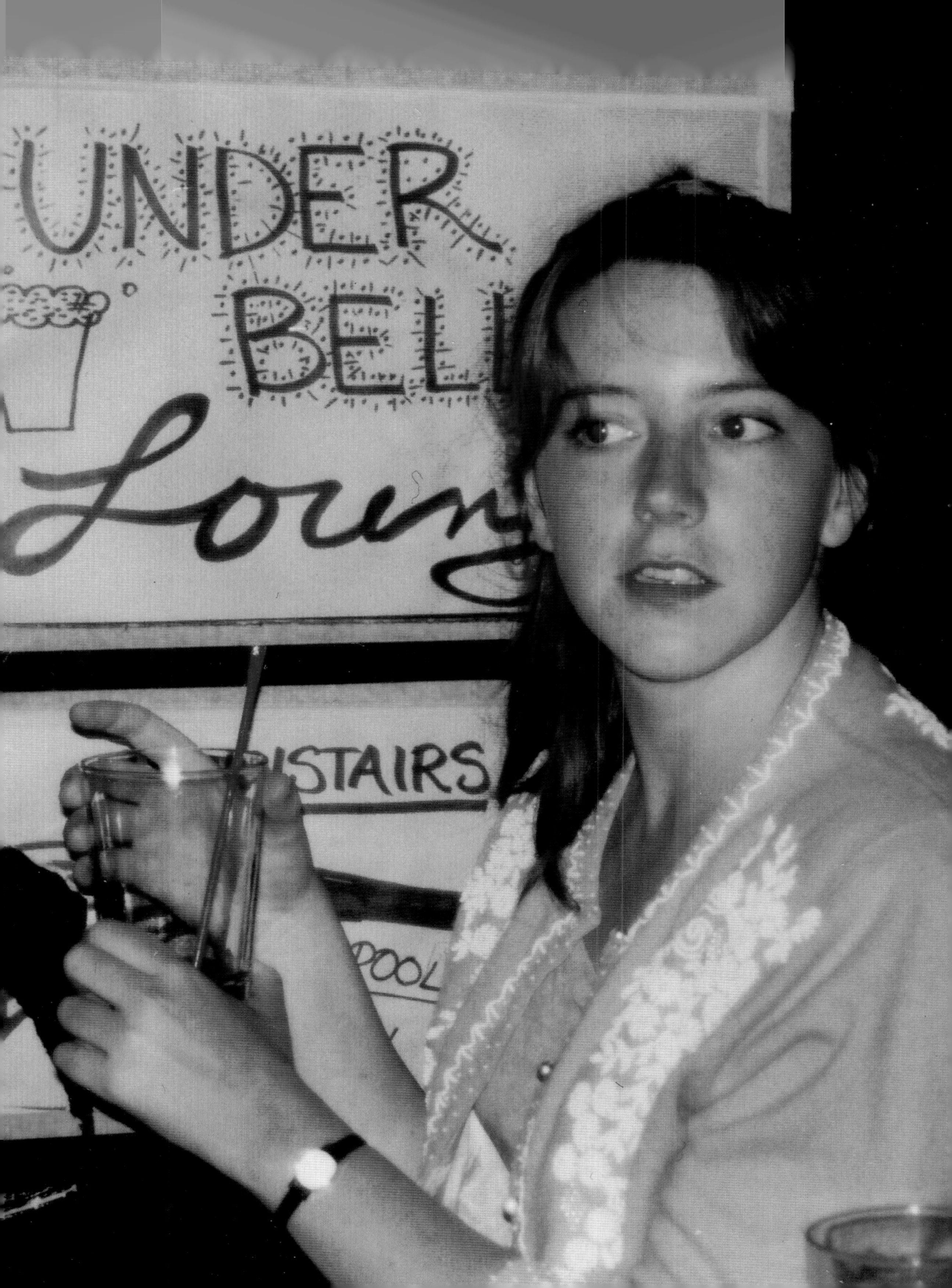
UNDER
STAIRS

Photo credits

Page 8, 13, 53: Eddie Duggan

Page 9, 14 top, 127, 180-1, 184 bottom, 185: Mick Mercer

Page 10 top, 12, 23, 54 top: Christian Cavallin

Page 10 bottom: Chris Low

Page 11, 54 bottom, 55 bottom, 58, 59, 71, 72 bottom right, 74, 134 top, 142 bottom: Malcolm Riviera

Page 14 bottom: Peter McArthur

Page 15 top: Jeremy Gibbs

Page 15 bottom: Brian Nevill

Page 16: Steve Lewis

Page 17: Wayne Howarth

Page 18: Sara Bor

Page 19, 22, 23, 36: Rich Gunter

Page 24-25: Anita Corbin www.visiblegirls.com

Page 26, 27, 40-41: Simon Clegg

Page 28 top: Mark Nick Jordan

Page 28 bottom, 39 bottom: Fiona McNeill

Page 29 top, 30-31, 45: Neil Anderson

Page 29 bottom, 42: Andy AKA Birmingham 81

Page 32, 33: Photos by (the late) Scott Piering contributed by Richard Scott

Page 34: David Newton

Page 35: Simon Neil

Page 37: Graham Macindoe

Page 38: Mark Flunder

Page 39 top, 43, 98, 104 top, 110 bottom, 165 top: Sarah MacHenry

Page 44: Stefanie Heinrich

Page 48, 49, 50 bottom, 51 top, 52: Mike Murphy

Page 50 top: Melodye Chisholm

Page 51 bottom: Peter Muise

Page 55 top: Mykel Board

Page 56, 57 top: K Saul

Page 57 bottom: Nick Hill

Page 60, 61 top and bottom: Lindsay Hutton

Page 62-63, 66-67, 72 top left: Julia Gorton

Page 68 top, 69 top and bottom, 78: Ben Tecumseh DeSoto

Page 68 bottom: Steve Housden

Page 70, 72 bottom left, 79: Alison Braun

Page 72 top right: Liz Ibarra

Page 73: Angela Jaeger

Page 75 top, 77: Tiffany Pruitt

Page 75 bottom: Rikki Ercoli

Page 76 and 143: Lloyd Wolf

Page 80-81: Bessie Oakley

Page 82-83: Karen Filter

Page 86-87, 94, 178 bottom: Chris Scott

Page 88 top: Dean

Page 88 bottom: Alan Milliner

Page 89 top: Contributed by Gina Davidson

Page 89 bottom: Lynne Sims

Page 92 top, 104 bottom, 106, 116, 177 top, 179, 198 top: Stephen McRobbie

Page 92 bottom: Bobby Gillespie

Page 93 top, 101: Karen Parker

Page 93 bottom: Ken Copsey

Page 95 top, 110 top: Bridget Duffy

Page 95 bottom: Dave Travis

Page 96-97: Mark Raison

Page 98 bottom, 105: Emma Anderson

Page 99 top, 176 top: Karen Boyd

Page 99 bottom: Susan Henderson

Page 100: Ming DeNasty

Page 102-103: Maria Harris

Page 105 bottom, 112, 116 top: Nick Allport

Untypical Girls

Published by Cicada Books Limited

Written by Sam Knee
Picture research by Sam Knee
Photography by individual contributors
as specified
Design by April

British Library Cataloguing-in-Publication Data.

A CIP record for this book is available from
the British Library.
ISBN: 978-1-908714-45-9

Printed in China

Acknowledgements

I would like to say a huge humbling thanks to the
following radically cool individuals who contributed
their precious time, personal photo archives and who
allowed this book to become a reality, not remain just
another far fetched fantasy…

Erik Bluhm (unofficial West Coast Untypical Girls
researcher), Julie Cafritz, Malcom Riviera, Gina
Davidson, Debsey Wykes, Ellie Moran, Michael
Galinsky, Erin Smith, Pat Graham, Kira Roessler,
Stephen Pastel and Paul Kelly.

Huge thanks also to Studio April, Ziggy Hanaor,
Eleonora Marton and Neil Kidgell. And to Lisa
Kidner, my partner in this world and beyond, for her
faith and love thru thick and thin.

꩜

Cicada Books Limited
48 Burghley Road
London NW5 1UE
E: cicadabooks@gmail.com
W: www.cicadabooks.co.uk